P9-EED-464

What Every Person Wants to Know About

Prayer

By Marilyn Hickey

Marilyn Hickey Ministries

P.O. Box 17340 • Denver, Colorado 80217

What Every Person Wants to Know About Prayer

All scriptures are quoted from the
King James Version of the Bible
unless otherwise indicated.

Printed in the United States of America

CONTENTS

Chapter One
Why Pray?

AND he spake a parable unto them to this end, that men ought always to pray, and not to faint (Luke 18:1).

God is calling the Body of Christ to prayer. Though this is not a new call, it is an urgent one that—like a newborn baby—demands *immediate* attention. As cancer, AIDS, economic uncertainty, suicide, violence, divorce, homelessness, and national disasters become a part of everyday life, people are desperately crying out for help. And there is only one answer—PRAYER!

In times past, the American Church has been called the "prayerless" Church by Christians overseas. We've spent millions of dollars sending missionaries to evangelize the uttermost parts of the world, but we've neglected one of the most fundamental teachings of the Bible: *". . . men ought always to pray, and not to faint."*

The Greek word for *faint* is *ekkakeho*, which means "to be weak, to fail (in heart)," or "to become weary." Prayer is the **key** to strengthen you when you feel like giving up. It will give you the faith to believe that God will intervene because

He hears your cries and is willing to move on your behalf.

No Warm Fuzzies

Prayer has a purpose. It's not just a warm, fuzzy feeling or words you utter to God when all else has failed. Prayer is intimate fellowship with God through His Son, Jesus Christ. Prayer gets results, it gets down to the core of a thing, and it is vital in the times in which we live. No longer will Christians be able to live successfully without prayer and "hope" that God will show up on the scene.

In my travels throughout the country, I've noticed many Christians feel very defeated in their walk with God. Some have even backslidden and are angry at God because they feel He failed them when they needed Him most. Hebrews 13:5 says God will neither leave you nor forsake you. A failure to get the desired results when you pray is an indication that there is a problem on the praying end (you), and not on the hearing end (God). Perhaps you are not praying according to God's will for you in that situation.

Unless your life is *built* upon more than casual communication with God, your house *will not* be able to successfully endure the storms of life currently facing you or those you will encounter in the days ahead (see Matthew 7:24-27).

Prayer is communicating with God. It can be as personal as talking to a friend and as intimate as becoming one flesh with your spouse. Proverbs 18:24 says, " . . . *there is a friend that sticketh closer than a brother.*" In John 15:14,15, Jesus says, *"Ye are my friends, . . . Henceforth I call you not servants; . . . I have called you friends; for all things that I have heard of my Father I have made known unto you."*

Friends share things with one another that they don't communicate to the general public. God desires that type of fellowship with you. He created you to commune with Him.

I believe all of us are in God's kingdom because someone prayed us in. Prayer is so powerful; it's a two-way communication system. It is not just a way for you to communicate with God; it's also God's way to communicate with you.

Many new Christians (and some who have been Christians for years) don't know how to pray, so they pattern their prayers after the prayers of others. But prayer is an expression of your individuality. For some, it is a way to release the stress and anxiety of a hectic lifestyle. To others, it's an avenue for remaining on track with God, to get solutions to problems, to rescue a loved one from the grips of hell, or to be refreshed in God's presence.

Kingdom Building

And all things, whatsoever ye shall ask in prayer, believing, ye shall receive (Matthew 21:22).

You don't get things from God because you want them, hope you'll get them, or talk about them. You get things because you pray for them. Matthew 21:22 says you should come before God and ask in prayer, believing that you'll receive. (See also Mark 11:24.)

I understand that the sun is 93 million miles from the earth and that the light from the next closest star to the earth takes four years to reach us. Yet, God is in heaven (above the moon, sun, and stars), and our prayers reach Him instantly. You can pick up your phone, send a telegram, write a letter, or fly on an airplane to visit someone, but there is no faster communication system than prayer. Sometimes you may even call a wrong or disconnected number, but when you call on God you never get a busy signal or a recording.

If you want to receive an answer to your prayers, you must pray the way God tells you to. *All* prayer should be directed to the Father in Jesus' name: *"And whatsoever ye shall ask in my name, that will I do, that the Father may be glo.:ified in the Son. If ye shall ask any thing in my name, I will do it"* (John 14:13,14.)

Once, my husband Wally and I purchased a lamp

8

for our daughter Sarah's room. I didn't want to read the instructions; I just wanted to look at the picture on the box and put the lamp together. Needless to say, I was unable to assemble the lamp without referring to the directions. Prayer works much in the same way. The more you follow the directions, the more results you're going to have. Since we want results when we pray, we need to pray to the Father in the name of His Son, Jesus.

Two Persons of the Trinity pray with you when you pray in Jesus' name. Not only does the Holy Spirit pray for you, but you also have Jesus praying for you, too:

> *And in the same way the Spirit also helps our weakness; for we do not know how to pray as we should, but the Spirit Himself intercedes for us with groanings too deep for words; and He who searches the hearts knows what the mind of the Spirit is, because He intercedes for the saints according to the will of God. And we know that God causes all things to work together for good to those who love God, to those who are called according to His purpose* (Romans 8:26-28 NAS).

> *Hence, also, He is able to save forever those who draw near to God through Him, since He always lives to make intercession for them* (Hebrews 7:25 NAS).

Think about this. The Bible says that in the mouth of two or three witnesses every word is established (see Matthew 18:16). When you pray to the Father according to His Word, the Holy Spirit prays in agreement with you because He prays God's Word, too. Since Jesus ever lives to make intercession for you, He's praying for you also. How many are praying God's will? Three. And in the mouth of two or three witnesses your prayer is established.

When you pray according to God's instructions, all of heaven is fighting for you. When the devil comes before God to accuse you, Jesus, your Attorney, is seated at the right hand of God, your Judge. So when the devil enters the courtroom, *everything* is stacked against him because God the Father is your Judge, and Jesus the Intercessor is your Attorney.

Romans 8:31 says, *". . . If God be for* [you], *who can be against* [you]?" God has stacked prayer together to work in your favor and to bring to pass His will in your life and the lives of those you are praying for. You have three witnesses when you pray and no force in hell can defeat you as you pray in faith, believing the Word can and will work for you.

Mountain-moving Faith

And it shall come to pass, that before they

call, I will answer; and while they are yet speaking, I will hear (Isaiah 65:24).

Call unto me, and I will answer thee, and shew thee great and mighty things, which thou knowest not (Jeremiah 33:3).

Prayer is not a religious exercise that you do as you're dozing off to sleep at night or as you're rushing to work in the morning. Once you've grasped the importance of prayer, it will become very difficult for the devil to defeat you. You will have the *assurance* in your spirit that regardless of what comes, you can pray and God *will* move in your behalf. Unlike your prayer attitude of the past, you will pray expecting results!

Faith, which is believing that the Word of God is true AND that it will work for you, is one of the major components to effective praying. The Bible says faith can move both God *and* mountains. (See Mark 11:22,23; Hebrews 11:6.) The eloquence of your prayers, the abundance of your tears, or the amount of time you spend screaming at the top of your voice will not cause God to move on your behalf.

Abraham Moved God by Faith

But without faith it is impossible to please him: for he that cometh to God must believe that he is, and that he is a rewarder of them that diligently seek him (Hebrews 11:6).

Diligence means "to search out, investigate, crave, demand, worship." Whenever I think of diligence in prayer, I think of Abraham. The Scripture says Abraham believed the promises (Word) of God and it was attributed to him as having right standing with God:

What shall we say then that Abraham our father, as pertaining to the flesh, hath found? For if Abraham were justified by works, he hath whereof to glory; but not before God. For what saith the scripture? Abraham believed God, and it was counted unto him for righteousness (Romans 4:1-3).

Abraham is known as the "father of faith." and is listed in Hebrews 11 in what is known as the "faith hall of fame." His prayer life and walk with God was such that he *knew* he could approach God in prayer and God *would* move in his behalf.

The intimacy of their relationship can be seen in Genesis 18 when God revealed to Abraham His decision to destroy Sodom and Gomorrah because of the sin of its inhabitants. Abraham's nephew, Lot, dwelled in the cities of the plain of Sodom (see Genesis 13:7-12). God knew Abraham would not want his nephew and his family destroyed, so He gave him an opportunity to intercede for them.

. . . but Abraham stood yet before the LORD. And Abraham drew near, and said, Wilt thou also destroy the righteous with the wicked?

Peradventure there be fifty righteous within the city: wilt thou also destroy and not spare the place for the fifty righteous that are therein? That be far from thee to do after this manner, to slay the righteous with the wicked: and that the righteous should be as the wicked, that be far from thee: Shall not the Judge of all the earth do right? And the LORD said, If I find in Sodom fifty righteous within the city, then I will spare all the place for their sakes. And Abraham answered and said, Behold now, I have taken upon me to speak unto the Lord, which am but dust and ashes: Peradventure there shall lack five of the fifty righteous: wilt thou destroy all the city for lack of five? And he said, If I find there forty and five, I will not destroy it. And he spake unto him yet again, and said, Peradventure there shall be forty found there. And he said, I will not do it for forty's sake. And he said unto him, Oh let not the Lord be angry, and I will speak: Peradventure there shall thirty be found there. And he said, I will not do it, if I find thirty there. And he said, Behold now, I have taken upon me to speak unto the Lord: Peradventure there shall be twenty found there. And he said, I will not destroy it for twenty's sake. And he said, Oh let not the Lord be angry, and I will speak yet but this once: Peradventure ten shall be found there. And he said, I will not destroy it for ten's sake. And the LORD went his way, as soon as he had left communing with Abraham: and Abraham returned unto his place (Genesis 18:22-33).

You, too, can learn to operate in Abraham's level of faith in prayer by applying some very fundamental Biblical truths. First, remember that you are made nigh (near) God through the blood Jesus shed at Calvary. It is your right and privilege as a child of God to seek Him in prayer and expect Him to hear and answer you:

. . . remember that you were at that time separate from Christ, excluded from the commonwealth of Israel, and strangers to the covenants of promise, having no hope and without God in the world. But now in Christ Jesus you who formerly were far off have been brought near by the blood of Christ . . . and (reconciled) *. . . to God through the cross, . . .* (Ephesians 2:12,13,16 NAS).

Second, God has given you the right to use the name of Jesus, which has authority over everything in the heavens and earth and beneath the earth: *"That at the name of Jesus every knee should bow, of things in heaven, and things in earth, and things under the earth, And that every tongue* should confess that Jesus Christ is Lord, . . . " (Philippians 2:10).

Third, you have the Holy Spirit guiding you: *"But when He, the Spirit of truth, comes, He will guide you into all the truth; . . . "* (John 16:13-15 NAS).

Fourth, enter God's presence with thanksgiving. Most of us approach the Lord with murmuring and complaints, but the Bible says we should, *" . . . Come before Him with joyful singing. Enter His gates with thanksgiving, And His courts with praise. Give thanks to Him; bless His name"* (Psalms 100:2,4 NAS).

When you bake bread, you put yeast in it so it will rise. When you enter into prayer to present your petitions before God with thanksgiving, your praise and thanksgiving to Him make your prayer requests rise into His presence.

Praying the Word of God is the fifth truth that is fundamental to prayer. Praying the promises of God (His Word) and not the problem guarantees results and brings the provisions that you need (see I John 5:14,15). You can state the problem: "Father, I'm in need of a financial blessing." But you must also pray His Word: *"Father, you say in Malachi 3:10 that because I bring my tithes and offerings into your storehouse that you will open the windows of heaven and pour me out a blessing that there shall not be room enough to receive it. So based on your Word, I thank you that this need is met. In Jesus' name. Amen."*

And sixth, you must depend on the Holy Spirit when you pray. Ephesians 3:20 tells of the tremendous power of the Holy Spirit at work within us. After you've come into God's courts with thanksgiving, praying the Word, you loose the *dunamis* (miracle-working power) of the Holy Spirit to get behind your prayers as He intercedes for you with groanings that cannot be uttered (Romans 8:26,27) and causes things in heaven and earth to line up so that your prayers will come to pass.

Chapter Two
Types of Prayer

I EXHORT therefore, that, first of all, supplications, prayers, intercessions, and giving of thanks, be made for all men (I Timothy 2:1).

One of the major reasons for unanswered prayer is that we lump all prayer in the same big package, not realizing that there are different types of prayer for different types of needs. When a child, for example, wants a piece of candy, his request is different than it would be if he had fallen and broken his leg or if he wanted to know which chore you wanted him to do first—clean his room or take out the trash.

As I mentioned in chapter one, you must follow God's directions for prayer if you expect to get results when you pray. Different recipes call for different ingredients. If you're going to make a pound cake, you don't add cottage cheese and pepper, nor do you boil an egg by putting it in a skillet to fry. So it is with prayer. If you want an effective prayer life, follow God's prayer manual—the Bible.

The apostle Paul had a good understanding of the different types of prayer. In I Timothy 2:1 he mentions supplications, prayers (which indicates prayers other than the ones listed), intercessions, and thanksgiving. Jesus also demonstrated different types of prayers during His earthly ministry. In the Garden of Gethsemane, he prayed a prayer of committal; at Lazarus' tomb, He prayed a prayer of thanksgiving; and in Matthew 18, He taught His disciples the prayer of binding and loosing and the prayer of agreement.

Prayer of Agreement

*. . . **if two of you shall agree on earth** as touching any thing that they shall ask, it shall be done for them of my Father which is in heaven. For where two or three are gathered together in my name, there am I in the midst of them.* (Matthew 18:19,20).

The prayer of agreement is a prayer in which two or more people set themselves in agreement with God's Word, one another, and Jesus, Who, according to this scripture, is in the midst of them.

Harmony is important. If you or the person(s) you're agreeing with in prayer are out of fellowship with the Lord or one another, or there is unforgiveness or strife in your life, it will bind the hands of God, hinder your prayers, and leave a door open for Satan to come in and steal, kill, or destroy (see Mark 11:25,26; Galatians 5:6; James 3:14,16).

Prayer of Binding and Loosing

*Verily I say unto you, Whatsoever ye shall **bind** on earth shall be bound in heaven: and whatsoever ye shall **loose** on earth shall be loosed in heaven* (Matthew 18:18).

The extent to which God is free to move in the earth and in your prayer life depends upon YOU! The prayer of binding (to knit or tie) and loosing (to break or destroy) can stop Satan in his tracks. This is "cause and effect" praying (i.e., you bind poverty and loose finances). Because you have the name of Jesus, which has authority over every thing that is named (cancer, lack, rebellion, etc.), you can hinder Satan's ability on earth to interfere with the will of God. So what things you tie (as in a knot) on earth, God will break or destroy in heaven.

Prayer of Petition and Supplication

*Be careful for nothing; but in every thing by **prayer and supplication** with thanksgiving let your requests be made known unto God. And the peace of God, which passeth all understanding, shall keep your hearts and minds through Christ Jesus* (Philippians 4:6,7).

The Amplified Bible says, *"Do not fret or have any anxiety about anything, but in every circumstance and in everything, by prayer and petition (definite requests), with thanksgiving, continue to make your wants known to God. And God's peace [shall be yours, . . .]."*

The only requirements for the prayer of petition and supplication are that you know what your request is before you approach God in prayer and that your request is based on the Word. It is so encouraging to know that you don't have to be nervous, worried, or uptight about anything. You can simply petition God and He will keep your heart and mind at peace.

United Prayer

*And being let go, they went to their own company, and reported all that the chief priests and elders had said unto them. And when they heard that, they **lifted up their voice to God with one accord,** . . . And when they had prayed, the place was shaken where they were assembled together; and they were all filled with the Holy Ghost, and they spake the word of God with boldness* (Acts 4:23,24,31).

The believers in the New Testament church knew the power of united prayer. Acts 12 describes a prayer meeting of a group of believers who were praying for the release of Peter who had been imprisoned for preaching the gospel. Verse 5 says *". . . prayer was made without ceasing of the **church** unto God for him."* The power of their united prayer was so great that God dispatched an angel to rescue Peter out of King Herod's clutches and an iron gate opened of its own accord. There is power when the Body of Christ comes together to pray, which is why believers are admonished to fellowship and attend church on a regular basis (see Hebrews 10:25).

Thanksgiving and Praise

*Enter into his gates with **thanksgiving,** and into his courts with **praise**:…* (Psalms 100:4).

Have you ever noticed how ineffective your prayers are and how burdened you feel when you do nothing but complain to God during your prayer time? When you enter into His courts with thanksgiving to present your petitions, like yeast causes dough to rise, thanksgiving makes your prayer requests rise into the presence of the Father, and it lifts you above the heaviness or hopelessness of your situation.

Prayer of Commitment

*Then cometh Jesus with them unto a place called Gethsemane . . . And he went a little farther, and fell on his face, and prayed, saying, O my Father, if it be possible, let this cup pass from me: nevertheless **not as I will, but as thou wilt*** (Matthew 26:36,39).

From Genesis to Revelation, the Bible is clear about what is and is not God's will. In Matthew 26,

Jesus is praying a prayer of commitment. It took three times for Him to totally submit to the will of God. He said, "Oh Lord, I don't want to drink this cup . . . If you will, let it pass from me." And finally, "Nevertheless, your will be done." Jesus agonized in prayer over this until He submitted to the will of His Father. (See verses 36-44). The prayer of commitment is the *only* time you should pray, "If it be thy will." Otherwise, you should find a Scripture to support your need and pray, "Your Word says . . . ."

Praying in the Spirit

*Now unto him that is able to do exceeding abundantly above all that we ask or think, according to the **power** that worketh in us, . . .* (Ephesians 3:20).

Praying in the Spirit releases the power of God to bring your prayers to pass. The Greek word for *power* in this Scripture is "dunamis"; it means "miracle-working power." When you are endued with miracle-working power you can go forth in prayer and attack the world for Jesus Christ because of the power at work within you.

Romans 8:26-28 says you do not know how to pray for things as you ought, but the Holy Spirit prays through you with groanings and utterances that cannot be thought out. Because the Holy Spirit searches the hearts of the people who are going to be involved in your situation, He makes intercession according to God's will. When you pray in the Spirit, God makes everything (including the hearts of men) come together according to His will.

Praying God's Word

*But he answered and said, **It is written,** Man shall not live by bread alone, but by every word that proceedeth out of the mouth of God* (Matthew 4:4).

Jesus beat the devil with the Word. You also must pray God's Word to defeat Satan. For every problem, you should pray a promise because it's the promise (the Word) that does not return void (see Isaiah 55:11). Praying God's Word accomplishes three things—it reminds God of His Word, it reminds the devil he is defeated, and it increases your faith because *" . . . faith cometh by hearing, and hearing by the word of God"* (Romans 10:17). Praying the Word brings the provisions that you need.

Chapter Three
The Lord's Prayer

After this manner therefore pray ye: Our Father which art in heaven, Hallowed be thy name. Thy kingdom come. Thy will be done in earth, as it is in heaven. Give us this day our daily bread. And forgive us our debts, as we forgive our debtors. And lead us not into temptation, but deliver us from evil: For thine is the kingdom, and the power, and the glory, for ever, Amen (Matthew 6:9-13).

Now that we have examined types of prayer, we need to go a little further and look at a "prayer pattern" that Jesus gave His disciples to follow. I'm sure many of you have recited this prayer at least once in your life, and even today some congregations sing it as one of their Sunday morning hymns. It is known as "The Lord's Prayer."

Sometimes you can figure out what something is by knowing what it is not. Jesus wanted to make sure His disciples knew the correct prayer method and had direction and purpose for what they wanted to accomplish in prayer . . . BEFORE they prayed.

25

In Matthew 6:7 He instructed His disciples **not** to pattern their prayers after the heathen because they did not know how or what to pray. They babbled the same thing over and over again, hoping they would say something that would move God. Then Jesus told them **how** to pray, *"After this manner therefore pray ye: . . . "* (verse 9).

Temples of the Holy Ghost

. . . know ye not that your body is the temple of the Holy Ghost which is in you, . . . ? (I Corinthians 6:19).

Throughout the Old Testament we see examples of God manifesting His presence in temples made by man (see II Chronicles 5:13,14). Upon Jesus' death and resurrection, God transferred the indwelling of His presence from man-made temples into earthen vessels. First Corinthians 6:19 says that you, as a New Testament believer, are the Temple of God and that the Holy Ghost (God's presence) dwells in you.

Matthew 21:12-16 draws an interesting parallel to this. In this account, Jesus went into the Temple and threw out the people who were peddling their wares, declaring the Temple to be a house of prayer: *"And Jesus went into the temple of God, and cast out all them that sold and bought in the temple, and overthrew the tables of the moneychangers, and the seats of them that sold doves, And said unto them, It is written, My house shall be called the house of prayer; . . . "* (verses 12,13).

There is an interesting progression that takes place in this passage of Scripture. If you'll notice, the first thing Jesus did was cleanse the Temple, and then He identified its purpose. The Temple's purpose was not for sin or unrighteousness—Jesus referred to it as a house of prayer. Once its purpose was identified and the cleansing took place, Jesus began healing the sick, the lame, and the blind, and then the children began to sing praises unto Him (verses 14,15).

As the Temple was a house of prayer during Old Testament times, so is every New Testament born-again believer. As Jesus cleansed the Temple in Matthew 21, He also wants to cleanse you of anything that could hinder the effectiveness of your prayers. The benefit to you when this process takes place is that God's power will begin to flow through you and YOU will begin to heal the lame, the sick, and the blind. YOU will become a house of praise (verse 16).

The prayer pattern outlined by Jesus in Matthew 6 will purify you and cause you to become a house of prayer and perfected praise. Jesus gave His disciples this prayer pattern so they could reap all the benefits of prayer. Each verse, or demarcation (a marker used to designate an athlete's arrival at a certain point in a marathon or a related sport) of this scripture will lead you into a different level of prayer. As you go through each point of demarcation, the Holy Spirit will show you how and what to pray.

The Lord's Prayer

. . . Our Father which art in heaven, Hallowed be thy name (Matthew 6:9).

This is the first point of demarcation. At this point you allow the Holy Spirit to unfold to you what He wants you to pray. When I pray this prayer, I get in tune with the Holy Spirit by saying, "Father, thank You that You are the God Who is more than enough. You are El Shaddai. Thank You for the name of Jesus. It's because of that name, the most hallowed name I know, that my sins have been forgiven. So I am cleansed with His blood. Because of His name, I have the Holy Spirit to lead me into truth. I don't have to live in depression, be deceived, or make mistakes. The Holy Spirit will lead me into all truth."

Then, wait on God. If you are sick, the Holy Spirit might have you pray, "Father, I thank You that because of Your hallowed name, I have health. Jesus Himself took my infirmities and my diseases. By His stripes, I am healed."

Depending on the needs of your life and the way the Holy Spirit is leading you that day, you may spend a long time at this demarcation, or He may move you to the next point.

Thy kingdom come . . . (verse 10).

At this point I begin by praying about my relationship with God. I might pray, "Father, I want to please You. If I have blown it in any area, or if there is something blocking our relationship, would You please show me by the Holy Spirit? Have I been ugly with my tongue? Critical? Prideful? Father, would You reveal it to me now by the Holy Spirit?"

Again, I wait upon the Lord for a moment to see how He is leading me. If He doesn't lead me to pray about anything else concerning my relationship with Him, then I begin praying over my relationship with my husband, Wally, and my children, Michael and Sarah. Then I move on to the next point of demarcation.

. . . Thy will be done in earth, as it is in heaven (verse 10).

God has a will for you in heaven for every relationship that you're involved in—your relationship with your heavenly Father, your mate, your children, and others. I might pray, "God, You have called me to Marilyn Hickey Ministries. You've called me to be a pastor's wife. Lord, show me what I should do for You today."

Perhaps the Holy Spirit will give me wisdom for a certain decision facing me that day, or perhaps

He will show me the face of someone in the church who needs prayer. I stay at this demarcation until the Holy Spirit directs me to the next point.

Give us this day our daily bread (verse 11).

The Holy Spirit could lead you to pray for daily bread in a lot of ways. With me, for example, I might be stuck on a topic I'm going to teach, so I pray for revelation knowledge: "Father would You give me revelation in Your Word concerning this topic?"

Perhaps you have a financial or physical need. Or maybe the Holy Spirit will lead you to pray for someone else. I've prayed for my mother for years: "Father, give my mother her daily bread. She's in her 80's and she needs daily health and strength. Meet her every need today."

And forgive us our debts, as we forgive our debtors (verse 14).

God wants you to have good relationships. When you're rude or vindictive to others, God can't bless you the way He wants to. So each day during my prayer time I say, "Father, I make the decision to forgive today and to walk in love toward others regardless of what they have done or may do to me. Please show me how to forgive according to Your Word."

And lead us not into temptation, but deliver us from evil: For thine is the kingdom, and the power, and the glory, for ever, Amen (verse 13).

Some Christians are tempted more than others because they don't pray. Jesus said to pray so you would not be tempted (see Matthew 26:41). Just as God has a perfect will for you each day, the devil has designed a device in hell for each day of your life to hinder the will of God for you that day.

I might pray, "Father, don't lead me into temptation but deliver me from evil for Thine is the kingdom, and the power (out of my "house of prayer" comes power), and the glory (praise) forever, Amen."

Chapter Four
Meditation

*But his delight is in the law of the LORD; and in his law doth he **meditate** day and night. And he shall be like a tree planted by the rivers of water, that bringeth forth his fruit in his season; his leaf also shall not wither; and whatsoever he doeth shall prosper* (Psalms 1:2,3).

Meditation can change your life! According to Psalms 1:2,3, meditating the Word of God guarantees prosperity for every born-again believer. In the book of Joshua, God confirmed His Word with the promise that if you will meditate on the Word, keeping it in your mouth and acting upon it, you will be successful in every area of your life— spiritually, physically, mentally, emotionally, and financially:

This book of the law shall not depart out of thy mouth; but thou shalt meditate therein day and night, that thou mayest observe to do according to all that is written therein: for then thou shalt make thy way prosperous, and then thou shalt have good success (Joshua 1:8).

Many people will say, "Well, that was only written for Joshua." But no matter what you do, obedience to Joshua 1:8 will bring *you* prosperity in all things. You will be the best you can be as a parent, spouse, child, cook, student—no matter what you do. This is a key scripture and carries a tremendous impact.

The word *meditate* has many meanings: to "walk, talk, memorize, visualize," and "personalize" the Word of God. Joshua 1:8 is God's command for His people to meditate on His Word. This command carries a promise that goes with everything in your life. God is saying, "If you will meditate on My Word day and night, speak that Word, and obey it in every area of your life, you will prosper AND be successful in *everything* you set your heart to do."

Threefold Cord

There is a three-part action plan in Joshua 1:8 that God has given for meditating on His Word. Part one involves your mouth: *"This book of the law shall not depart out of thy **mouth**."* Remember, meditation involves "talking" God's Word.

Part two is meditation itself: *". . . but thou shalt meditate therein **day and night**, ..."* Meditation on God's Word is to be an all-consuming effort, not merely a pastime.

Part three brings in the action: *". . . that thou*

*mayest observe to **do** according to all that is written therein . . . ."* Meditation not only involves speaking—it involves walking. We are to be doers of the Word and not hearers only (see James 1:22).

God did not say, "If you'll do this, **I'll** make your way prosperous." He said, "If you'll meditate, **you** will make your way prosperous and you will have good success." There is a big difference here. You alone make the decision. God will not force you to meditate upon His Word; neither will He force prosperity upon you.

You may know people, perhaps unsaved people, who, according to the world's standards, are successful. But according to this scripture, there is a "good" success that comes with meditating the Word. This success has to do with more than material possessions—it covers every aspect of your life and can be passed on to your future generations (see Deuteronomy 7:9).

When God told Joshua to meditate, He was saying, "I want you to be saturated with the Word of God: keep it in your mind, your mouth, and your actions." Joshua became an example of God's living Word in action—and so can you!

When I first started to meditate on the Word, I decided that I needed a partner. I thought that in case I wanted to stop meditating or became discouraged, a partner would be an encouragement to me. This seemed a good way to start, so I prayed, "Lord, with whom would you have me be a partner?" The Lord spoke to me, and it was not the person I wanted Him to choose! She was a person who griped constantly. If she got ahold of you, it would take 30 minutes for her to tell you her problems; and then she'd find you later because she had more to tell!

The Lord said to me, "I want her to be your meditation partner." I thought, "Oh Lord, anybody but her." I thought she would spend the time griping and that we wouldn't get through the verses. Then I thought, "Oh, she'll say 'no.'" So I called her and said, "For the rest of my life (to entrap myself in a commitment to the Lord), I'm going to meditate on the Word of God. I'll start in Proverbs, and I would like you to be my partner for that book."

She agreed, and I made arrangements to call her at 7 a.m. each day. I also told her that I wouldn't be able to talk for very long because I had to get my children ready for school.

The next morning when I called her she immediately started griping.

"Let's go over our verses," I told her.

"No," she said, "I need to tell you this first. I am just so depressed."

"Well, I don't have time because my children have to get to school," I said. Then we went over our Bible verses. For the next two weeks, every time I called, this lady wanted to gripe, but I didn't have time for griping. We would go over the meditated scriptures and that was all.

When the third week began, something had happened. I called her and instead of griping she said, "I got the most marvelous thing out of this chapter! Did you get this?" She then shared the revelation she had received from the Word. It was so exciting! Her whole attitude turned around from that day on.

One day, some time afterward, my husband asked me, "What happened to that woman? She used to be the most negative person I'd ever seen."

I said, "I can tell you what happened to her. The Word of God started coming out of her mouth through meditation and it **changed** her!"

Foundation for Meditation

The three basic steps to meditation are *memorization,* *personalization,* and *visualization.*

The first step is *memorization.* In John 14:26 Jesus promised to send the Holy Spirit Who would bring "all things" that Jesus said to your remembrance. The Holy Spirit can't bring something to your remembrance if there is nothing there to draw from. You are to memorize God's Word so that He can make you remember.

Personalization is the next step to meditation. As you meditate, don't just say, "This is God's Word to all Christians." Instead say, "This is God's Word for ME." Some people read the Bible as though it's for everybody but themselves. God is no respecter of persons—His promises are for YOU! (See Acts 10:34.) Personalize each scripture by putting your name or the names of your loved ones in place of the words, you, he, she, they, them, etc.

The last step of meditation involves *visualization*. To visualize the Word means that you must **see** God's Word as coming to pass in your life in spite of what circumstances may look like. Visualization can be called "faith sight"— you see it as yours through the eyes of faith (see Romans 4:17). Visualization is first found in Genesis 22. Hebrews 11 gives you the New Testament version of what occurred:

By faith Abraham, when he was tried, offered up Isaac: and he that had received the promises offered up his only begotten son, Of whom it was said, That in Isaac shall thy seed be called: Accounting that God was able to raise him up, even from the dead; from whence also he received him in a figure (verses 17-19).

When you meditate on the Word, begin saying what God says; begin to accept His Word as a reality in your life. Visualize it coming to pass for you.

Meditating on the Word is one of the most important things you can do as a Christian. When you set your priorities upon meditation, every area of your life will be transformed. It worked for Joshua in the Old Testament, and it will work for you today!

Chapter Five
Intercessory Prayer

*I EXHORT therefore, that, first of all, supplications, prayers, **intercessions,** and giving of thanks, be made for all men; For kings, and for all that are in authority; that we may lead a quiet and peaceable life in all godliness and honesty. For this is good and acceptable in the sight of God our Saviour; Who will have all men to be saved, and to come unto the knowledge of the truth* (I Timothy 2:1-4).

We live in an "instant" society—instant coffee, instant tea, instant pudding—and many of us want instant answers to our prayers. We have no problem *waiting* to hear from God as long as it only takes five seconds, minutes, or days. However, when we have to wait *five months* or **five years** for an answer to prayer, many of us grow fainthearted and say, "Forget it!"

God wants us to travail in prayer as a woman travails in childbirth. All too often we miss the reward He has for us because we lack stick-to-it-iveness in prayer. I have often taught that we should "play" until we win. Well, we should also

41

"pray" until we win.

Exodus 32-34 gives a beautiful example of someone who prayed until he won with God, a person used by God as a powerful intercessor. An *intercessor* is one who acts in the behalf of someone in difficulty or trouble. He pleads or petitions someone on their behalf, or attempts to reconcile differences between two people or groups—a mediator.

Intercession is the will of God. In I Timothy 2:1-3, the Apostle Paul lists three groups of people we should intercede for. He begins by being very general and saying we should intercede for *all* men, and then he narrows it to kings (political leaders), and for all who are in authority (pastors, policemen, employers, parents, teachers, etc.).

The two benefits of intercession, according to this scripture, are that it will enable us to live godly and honest lives in peace and quiet, free from a society of stress, crime, violence, and fear, and that men will surrender their hearts to God and come into the knowledge of His saving grace.

There is *tremendous* power in intercessory prayer. Although you may not intercede for others as a lifestyle, I Timothy 2 *commands* all born-again believers to pray the prayer of intercession in much the same way you would pray a prayer of thanksgiving, or of petition and supplication.

Priests of Intercession

Moses was a mighty intercessor. God called him to lead the Israelites out of Egypt and into the Promised Land (see Exodus 3). In fulfilling God's call, Moses saved an entire *nation* from destruction through the prayer of intercession.

When God first called him, Moses didn't feel he had the proper credentials. Moses asked God, *". . . Who am I, that I should go unto Pharaoh, and that I should bring forth the children of Israel out of Egypt?"* (Exodus 3:11).

God assured Moses that He would be with him and explained *how* He was going to deliver the Israelites from Egyptian bondage. That was not enough for Moses, however. In verse 13 he asked God, "Who are You?" God responded, *". . . I AM THAT I AM: . . . say unto the children of Israel, The LORD God of your fathers, the God of Abraham, the God of Isaac, and the God of Jacob, hath sent me unto you: . . . "* (Exodus 3:14,15).

Moses was still not convinced. As a child in Pharaoh's house, he had been trained to depend on his own abilities and intellect and hadn't learned the Source of his strength. Although he was a powerful speaker in Pharaoh's household and is described in Acts 7:22 as being *" . . . mighty in words and in deeds,"* Moses had lost his confidence after he murdered an Egyptian and the Israelites rejected his leadership (see

Exodus 2:11-14). He assured God that he would fail because he was *". . . slow of speech, and of a slow tongue"* (Exodus 4:10).

If you remember, God became upset with Moses and appointed his brother, Aaron, as his mouthpiece. However, as Moses' relationship with God and his confidence grew, Moses pushed Aaron aside and began interceding for the children of Israel himself.

Israel Didn't Know God

The Israelites were a carnal people and were accustomed to worshipping idols. Psalms 103:7 says Moses knew God's *ways* and the Israelites' knew His *acts*. They didn't have a personal relationship with God, nor did they have a Bible to live by. They were dominated by their minds, wills, and emotions.

In Exodus 32 the Israelites had grown impatient because 40 days had passed and Moses hadn't come down from Mount Sinai where he was communing with God. They depended on Moses to hear from God and to provide leadership. Believing he had deserted them, the Israelites rebelled and talked Aaron into making a golden calf for them to worship. Perhaps, they thought, the calf would provide some direction.

Meanwhile on Mount Sinai, Moses was having a marvelous time. God had given him specific instructions and had written the Ten Commandments on stone tablets for him to deliver to the Israelites. But on the fortieth day of their fellowship, God said to Moses: *". . . Go, get thee down; for **thy people,** which **thou broughtest out** of the land of Egypt, have corrupted themselves"* (Exodus 32:7).

The Israelites' had a history of murmuring and transgressing against God and had even angered God and Moses on several occasions, but this was the first time God had disowned them and was ready to destroy them:

They have turned aside quickly out of the way which I commanded them: they have made them a molten calf, and have worshipped it, and have sacrificed thereunto, and said, These be thy gods, O Israel, which have brought thee up out of the land of Egypt. And the LORD said unto Moses, I have seen this people, and, behold, it is a stiffnecked [rebellious] *people: **Now therefore let me alone,** that my wrath may wax hot against them, and that I may consume them: and I will make of thee a great nation* (Exodus 32:8-10).

Moses entered into immediate intercession for the Israelites. Although God had told him to leave Him alone so He could destroy Israel, Moses (and God) knew Moses could change God's mind and save a nation through his intercession.

Moses could have said, "Go ahead and kill them. I can't stand being around this crowd anyway." Instead, he chose to stand between the Lord's wrath and the Israelites. He refused to claim the Israelites as his people—he reminded God that they belonged to Him. Moses appealed to God's grace and reminded Him that He would hurt His own reputation if He destroyed the Israelites:

And Moses besought the LORD his God, and said, LORD, why doth thy wrath wax hot against thy people, which thou hast brought forth out of the land of Egypt with great power, and with a mighty hand? Wherefore should the Egyptians speak, and say, For mischief did he bring them out, to slay them in the mountains, and to consume them from the face of the earth? Turn from thy fierce wrath, and repent of this evil against thy people (Exodus 32:11,12).

Moses also appealed to God using His Word. "Now God," he said, "I am not the only seed of Abraham, Isaac, and Jacob—the Israelites are their seed, too. If You wipe them out, You will be going back on Your Word." (See Exodus 32:13,14.)

God reclaimed the Israelites, but they did not get away with their transgression. Although Moses interceded for them and changed the outcome of God's wrath, they were still held accountable for what they had done:

> *Then Moses stood in the gate of the camp,
> and said, Who is on the LORD'S side? let
> him come unto me. And all the sons of Levi
> gathered themselves together unto him. And
> he said unto them, Thus saith the LORD God
> of Israel, Put every man his sword by his
> side, and go in and out from gate to gate
> throughout the camp, and slay every man
> his brother, and every man his companion,
> and every man his neighbor. And the children
> of Levi did according to the word of Moses:
> and there fell of the people that day about
> three thousand men* (Exodus 32:26-28).

We can change the outcome of the world
through intercessory prayer. Moses saved an entire
nation. The 3,000 people who lost their lives did
so only because they *chose* not to repent. Had
they repented, all of Israel would have been spared.
Once Moses had brought the people to repentance
and destroyed those who wouldn't, he returned
to God on Mount Sinai to restore the Israelites'
fellowship with God:

> . . . *Oh, this people have sinned a great sin,
> and have made them gods of gold. Yet now,
> if thou wilt forgive their sin—; and if not,
> blot me, I pray thee, out of thy book which
> thou hast written* (Exodus 32:31,32).

Moses was a true intercessor. He told God that

if He would not forgive the Israelites, then he wanted to be blotted out of the Lamb's Book of Life right along with them. Because of his steadfastness, Moses prevailed in prayer and God consented to his request.

"All right, Moses," God said, "I will only blot out those who sinned against me. You'll get to go into the Promise Land, BUT I will not go with you. I will send an angel before you to lead you in."

Up until this point, God had never said He would send His angel before the Israelites. His presence in the form of a cloud or a pillar of fire had always led them, and He had promised Moses that His presence would go before them into the Promise Land. Moses refused to accept anything less than what God had initially promised. He continued in intercession:

And Moses said unto the LORD, See, thou sayest unto me, Bring up this people: and thou hast not let me know whom thou wilt send with me. Yet thou hast said, I know thee by name, and thou hast also found grace in my sight. Now therefore, I pray thee, if I have found grace in thy sight, shew me now thy way, that I may know thee, that I may find grace in thy sight: and consider that this nation is thy people. And he said, My presence shall go with thee, ... (Exodus 33:12-14).

Moses interceded until he changed the heart of God. I've seen people hold on to God for 20, 30, or 40 years and only now are seeing the manifestation of what they've interceded for. They never let go of God in prayer—they held on and got what they were praying for.

Something very glorious happened to Moses as he interceded for the Israelites. As he continued seeking God on their behalf, his heart became knitted to theirs and they became one. He began to esteem their well being and their salvation more than his own. He was willing to lose God's presence for their sakes and be eternally damned.

Intercessory prayer is imperative in the times in which we live. If you are willing to intercede or mediate between God and man, then through YOUR intercession you can change the heart of God and save a soul, a city, a state, and, who knows, perhaps a nation.

Chapter Six
Prayer and Fasting

*Is not this **the fast that I have chosen?** to loose the bands of wickedness, to undo the heavy burdens, and to let the oppressed go free, and that ye break every yoke?* (Isaiah 58:6).

Prayer and fasting go together. If you have never fasted before, the thought of denying yourself one or more meals may sound like a drudgery or something to avoid. Fasting, however, is yet another tool to help you experience breakthroughs in prayer. Fasting that is Spirit-inspired can be quite rewarding and as easy as 1-2-3.

Many people fast to diet, and although I'm not against losing weight, I am against it being your goal in fasting. If losing weight is your purpose in fasting, you will miss the fullness of the reason for fasting.

I had always associated fasting with a long, long period of time. However, you can fast just one meal and still allow God to do some wonderful things in your life.

My husband, Wally, had never been taught fasting. When he first began serving the Lord he had a friend in a mental hospital about whom he was very concerned. As he prayed for his friend, the Lord spoke to him, *"Howbeit this kind goeth not out but by **prayer and fasting"*** (Matthew 17:21).

Wally didn't know anything about fasting, but he fasted one meal. He was thrilled that even after such a short fast, the man was released from the hospital in his right state of mind!

As we study this chapter about prayer and fasting, I don't want you to think about the length of time you should fast, but how you can reap the most benefits out of your times of prayer *and* fasting.

Spirit-led Fasting

Jesus was spiritually prepared before His Father led Him to fast for 40 days. Matthew 4:1 says, *"Then was Jesus led up of the Spirit into the wilderness to be tempted of the devil."*

Regardless of the duration of your fast, you need to be led by the Holy Spirit. That is why Jesus could endure 40 days of fasting. Fasting for that length of time on your own could kill you if you are not Spirit-led. Let the Lord lead you in setting up a time frame for fasting.

In I Kings 18 and 19, God sent an angel to prepare the prophet Elijah for a 40-day fast. Elijah was very defeated at the time God called him to fast. He had just called down fire at Mount Carmel and had a tremendous victory. He had instructed the Israelites to kill the prophets of Baal and rolled them down the mountain, and God had opened the heavens in response to Elijah's prayer for rain. Then, because he had a supernatural anointing of strength, Elijah ran before Ahab's chariot into Jezreel (see I Kings 18).

When he arrived in Jezreel, he was greeted with a message from Ahab's wife, Jezebel: "I'm going to kill you," she said. Elijah immediately became fearful and ran into the wilderness and told God he had enough. (See I Kings 19:4).

Just as God had sent angels to minister to Jesus during His time of need in the wilderness in Matthew 4, He sent an angel to minister to Elijah in his moment of weakness: *"And as he lay and slept under a juniper tree, behold, then an angel touched him, and said unto him, Arise and eat. And he arose, and did eat and drink, and went in the strength of that meat forty days and forty nights unto Horeb the mount of God"* (I Kings 19:5,8).

In his attempt to escape Jezebel's wrath, Elijah went from a place of great faith and power to overwhelming fear. Fasting enabled him to get back into the realm of faith so he could hear from God:

. . . And, behold, the LORD passed by, and a great and strong wind rent the mountains, and brake in pieces the rocks before the LORD; but the LORD was not in the wind: and after the wind an earthquake; but the LORD was not in the earthquake: And after the earthquake a fire; but the LORD was not in the fire: and after the fire a still small voice (I Kings 19:11,12).

Because of his fast, Elijah was set free of thoughts of fear and unbelief. He was then able to take his eyes off the spectacular, and quiet his spirit to hear God's still, small voice.

Benefits of Fasting

Fasting will destroy the strongholds of unbelief in your life that can prevent you from operating in faith. In Matthew 17, Jesus was led by the Spirit to fast. He had been on the Mount of Transfiguration with three of His disciples, and when He descended, a man whose son was demon possessed came to Him and said, *". . . I brought him to thy disciples, and they could not cure him"* (verse 16).

Jesus prayed for the man's son, and he was delivered. When His disciples asked Him why they couldn't cast out the demons, Jesus answered and said, "You couldn't do it because of your unbelief. If you would fast and pray, you could cast out the demons because it would put you in a higher realm of faith." (See Matthew 17:20,21.)

Unbelief has to do with your ability to reason away the Word of God using your intellect. When you fast, your mind "shuts down" and your spirit begins to take control. This enables you to hear God's voice more clearly and operate in a higher level of faith. If the disciples had been fasting and praying, they would have been able to cast out the demons just as Jesus had done. Instead, the boy remained bound by the demons and the disciples were powerless over them.

Fasting and prayer will not only destroy unbelief, it will also break the powers of darkness over individuals, situations, cities, and nations. If you don't see results after standing on the Word and praying, you need to fast *and* pray.

A man once told me how God had called him to pastor a certain church. He contacted one of the most spiritually gifted men of that time and asked him, "Should I go? I feel like the Lord is calling me there." The man of God responded, "No. That place is simply overpowered with darkness—it's the worst place in the United States to go. It's a graveyard for preachers."

The pastor returned to the Lord and prayed, "Lord, here is a man of God saying not to go." The Lord said, "But I'm telling you to go."

The pastor obeyed God and pastored in this

town for 10 years but couldn't seem to accomplish anything. In desperation, he took control of the situation and went to Chicago to apply for another church. While in Chicago, the Lord spoke to him and said, "What are you doing here? I called you to another area."

The pastor answered, "God, I'm failing there. I'm tired of that area. I've tried everything for 10 years and nothing has worked, so I'm going to make a change."

God said, "You'll be out of My will."

The pastor answered, "Well, I seem to not be in Your will there!"

Then God told him, "You're in My will, but you need to go back and call your church to fast and pray." The pastor returned to the town and began a tremendous prayer and fasting program, and within two years his church grew from 200 to 2,000 people.

Prayer and fasting broke the powers of darkness over his city, and once those powers were broken, the pastor experienced a tremendous church explosion!

As I've already stated, prayer and fasting will help you hear from God more clearly. If you need an answer and feel you've done everything but the answer still has not come, then seek God's wisdom through prayer and fasting.

King Jehoshaphat found himself in a difficult

situation in II Chronicles 20. Three nations were getting ready to invade Israel and he was deeply concerned. Scripture says he became fearful and proclaimed a fast throughout all Judah. He said, "Fast with me, because we could be destroyed." The people began to fast and pray about their situation, and the Spirit of God moved on the prophet, Jahaziel:

And he said, Hearken ye, all Judah, and ye inhabitants of Jerusalem, and thou king Jehoshaphat, Thus saith the LORD unto you, Be not afraid nor dismayed by reason of this great multitude; for the battle is not your's, but God's. Ye shall not need to fight in this battle: set yourselves, stand ye still, and see the salvation of the LORD with you, O Judah and Jerusalem: fear not, nor be dismayed; to morrow go out against them: for the LORD will be with you (II Chronicles 20:15,17).

Then God gave Jehoshaphat the most unusual battle plan: *"And when he had consulted with the people, he appointed singers unto the LORD, and that should praise the beauty of holiness, as they went out before the army, and to say, Praise the LORD; for his mercy endureth for ever. And when they began to sing and to praise, the LORD set ambushments against the children of Ammon, Moab, and mount Seir, which were come against Judah; and they were smitten"* (II Chronicles 20:21,22).

Another benefit of prayer and fasting is that it will change you on the inside and cause you to focus on people other than yourself. If you trace Moses' life from beginning to end, you will discover that he was a hot-tempered egotist who, through prayer and fasting, became a meek and humble man. I've watched people with personality problems—hot tempers, immaturity, etc.—who manifest the fruit of the Spirit through consistent fasting and praying (see Galatians 5:22,23).

Ways to Fast

The most important thing you should remember when it comes to fasting is that you must be honest with God. If you have any unrepented sin or are involved in any kind of strife, your fasting and praying will not be effective (Isaiah 58:9,13). When you fast, do it in secret (Matthew 6:16-18); make sure your motivation for fasting is right and do not fast for selfish reasons (Isaiah 58:3,4).

How Long?

If God tells you to go on a three-day fast and you have that witness in your spirit, do it. If He speaks to you to go on a fast for one, seven, or 10 days, obey. It is good to be led by the Spirit in fasting.

The best kind of fasting, however, is consistent

fasting. It is easy to fast when you want to get out of trouble. If you consistently fast and pray, however, you could stay in a place of victory so when a potential problem arises, you will be so full of the Word and the Spirit that it will not become a crisis. You will already be prepared.

God's Promise to You

If you have never fasted, I suggest you begin. It will help you spiritually. Areas in which you've been defeated will become areas of victory for you, and you will begin to know how to better intercede and pray.

When you are Spirit-led in your fasting, not only will others be set free, but you will also reap certain benefits: God's compassion will begin to flow through you as you extend mercy to others; revelation knowledge, health, and divine protection are guaranteed; the Lord will guide you continually and you will never suffer lack; and you will experience a restoration as things that have been promised for generations will begin coming to pass. (See Isaiah 58:7,8,10-12.)

Types of Fast

There are three types of fast. The first is total abstinence—without food or water (see Matthew 4:2). I would advise against going on a fast without food *and* water. It could be physically dangerous, and I do not suggest that you do it unless God directs you.

The second is abstinence from food. Fasting is simply not eating. Don't try to put yourself on a long fast until you are ready. Let the Holy Spirit lead you. It is much more important that you fast consistently each week, even if it is only one meal which you set aside to fast unto the Lord. Also, make sure you use that time to pray. Whatever time you set aside to fast and pray, God will bless it.

Daniel's fast is the third type of fast. The Word says he "ate no pleasant meat" (see Daniel 10:3). Some people think this means giving up baked goodies. Although it's not known for sure, I think Daniel's fast was a vegetable diet—a fast of juices, fruits, and vegetables.

Being a spiritual Christian doesn't depend on you drinking juice or abstaining from food. You need to get the mind of Christ for your own fasting and prayer life. Just make sure you are consistent, making a dedication and consecration to the Lord.

Begin your week with fasting. Make a consecration today about how much you will fast during the week, then begin. Be consistent. Remember that fasting and prayer are twins—don't divide them; keep them together and you will have the most effective prayer life you have ever had!

Chapter Seven
Prayers That Change Nations

Ask of me, and I shall give thee the heathen
for thine inheritance, and the uttermost parts
of the earth for thy possession (Psalms 2:8).

In I Timothy 2:1,2 Paul admonishes the Body of Christ to make supplications, prayers, intercessions, and giving of thanks for all men, especially for leaders of nations (kings and those who are in authority). You may ask yourself, "Why should I pray for our nation's leaders?" The answer is quite simple: because the Bible says you can ask God for the heathen and the uttermost part of the earth for your possession. You may never visit another country or serve as a missionary, but God wants to use YOU to influence nations. How? Through your prayers and intercession.

As a Christian you have a responsibility to the nations of the world. The Bible shows that from the beginning of creation God has been concerned about nations, and you should be too. From the moment God created Adam and Eve, He has been watching out for and looking over people. After the fall, Adam's descendants began to replenish the earth, yet there is no reference to nations or countries until after the flood.

The Nations Begin

Genesis 10:32 says that God used individuals to build nations. Each of Noah's sons became fathers of nations. Shem's family multiplied and his descendants were the line from which the Jewish and Arab nations were born. Japheth's descendants "nationalized" the Indo-European countries; and Ham's descendants formed the African nations.

Shem's son, Eber, then had two sons: *". . . the name of one was Peleg; for in his days was the earth divided; and his brother's name was Joktan . . . . after their generations, in their nations: and by these were the nations divided in the earth after the flood"* (Genesis 10:25,32).

A better example of nations deriving from individuals comes from Genesis 12:2,3. God told Abraham He would make of Abraham a great nation and through him all the nations of the earth would be blessed. You see, God wanted a nation of His own. God's original plan was to start with just one man, then that man's descendants would become a nation of priests and take the Word of God to the world. He chose the seed of Abraham to be that nation. But by the time the Israelites left Egypt, they were a nation of murmurers instead of priests!

While in the wilderness the Israelites really blew it. They rebelled against God and built a golden calf. God told Moses He wanted to blot them out and start a new nation with Moses; but Moses interceded for Israel, and God spared them.

When the Israelites entered Canaan, God gave them opportunity to bring the light of God's truth to another nation. That meant the Israelites were to be priests to the ungodly, sinful Canaanites. God hoped that by putting a nation of priests with a nation of sinners and idol worshipers, the sinners would be saved. In fact, we know that some were saved—Rahab, her family, and the Gibeonites.

However, the Israelites became like the Canaanites, worshiping false gods and serving idols rather than the one, true God. They now needed a priest themselves; God chose a family from among the Jewish people—the tribe of Levi—to be priests to the Jewish nation and to keep them in line. But God didn't give up on His plan. God started over again with another individual, One Who was perfect in every way and would not fail—Jesus.

God did something very special that affected you and me. As individuals we are part of a nation—not the United States or Canada or Russia. Every individual who has professed a belief in Jesus Christ has become a citizen of the nation of God—God's kingdom. Peter tells us: *"But ye are a chosen generation, a royal priesthood, an holy nation, a peculiar people; that ye should shew forth the praises of him who hath called you out of darkness into his marvellous light"* (I Peter 2:9).

That means that you and I are now God's nation of priests! Just as it was God's original intent for the Jewish nation to be a nation of priests who would bring God's light to the other nations of the world, every Christian in the world, no matter where he or she lives, is to shine forth God's light to the world. ***We have become the nation of priests God has always wanted.***

Border Crossings

Now let's go back to another historical aspect of nations. As we already saw, Noah's descendants settled in different parts of the world and formed nations. Then *". . . the most High divided to the nations their inheritance, when he separated the sons of Adam, he set the bounds of the people according to the number of the children of Israel"* (Deuteronomy 32:8). God Himself determined the boundaries of nations!

Have you ever noticed that when men try to conquer other men's nations, their victory doesn't last very long? The "Nation of Islam" tried to conquer all of Europe, and even succeeded for a while—but God had a boundary on what these descendants of Shem could take. When Napoleon,

Hitler, and Communism tried to conquer the "world," they failed because they were exceeding the bounds set by God for their dominion. God starts a nation with an individual; and as descendants increase, He sets forth boundaries to establish the perimeters of the land on which they are to live.

But the seed of Abraham knows no boundaries. The citizens of God's nation are scattered around the world because the kingdom of God cannot be bound. God has priests in every corner of the world. Even when countries attempt to blot out Christianity, God knows how to get His priests into those countries. You don't actually have to travel to another country to affect it. Royal priests can remain in their own nations and have an impact on other nations.

You don't have to bring gifts to a country leader to bring conversion to the heathens of the world. Why? Because you are a citizen of a supernatural nation and you can travel by prayer. Your prayers can topple Communism, Nazism, Socialism, and any other "ism." Your prayers can open doors of countries that are locked up tight and bound by centuries of traditions. In fact, your prayers can "beget" a whole nation of believers! There are no "illegal aliens" in God's kingdom or from His kingdom because prayer is your passport to the world.

The mother-in-law of Dr. David Yonggi Cho—the Korean pastor of the world's largest church—told of her burden to pray for her own nation of South Korea after the Korean War. God told her to go to the border between North and South Korea, dig a hole in the mountain, and pray for six hours a day for about a month.

At the end of her prayer siege, she had a vision of a huge dragon in the sky that kept getting bigger and bigger. She thought, "Oh! It's North Korea, and the devil is going to come down and attack us." But she cried to God, rebuked the beast, and persevered in prayer. As the vision continued, she began to swell up until she was bigger than the dragon; then she "exploded" and the dragon exploded on top of her. God told her that North Korea would not come down and attack South Korea and that *her prayers had made the difference.* Like Dr. Cho's mother-in-law, who knows what work of the devil you are going to explode because you stand fast and pray for a nation?

Not only are you a priest, you are a royal priest, born again in royalty. That makes you a king. As a king of the nation of God, you have authority over worldly kings (leaders of nations). Through prayer and intercession you can bind ungodly actions of an earthly leader and loose what God wants to do in that leader's nation. You can decree

Psalms 2:8 and proclaim that nation to be a nation of intercessors and prayer warriors for the kingdom of God.

Chapter Eight
Unanswered Prayer

*And when ye stand praying, **forgive,** if ye have ought against any: that your Father also which is in heaven may forgive you your trespasses. But if ye do not forgive, neither will your Father which is in heaven forgive your trespasses* (Mark 11:25,26).

Now that we've familiarized ourselves with the "who, what, when, where, and why" of prayer, let's examine some attitudes and behaviors that could hinder or aid God in answering us when we call.

In Mark 11:24,25 Jesus is explaining to His disciples how to have mountain-moving faith. He encourages them to believe that whatever they "say" shall come to pass as long as they don't doubt in their hearts. He tells them their prayers will be so powerful that they will be able to speak to mountains and the mountains will have to move!

Then, almost as an afterthought, Jesus admonishes the disciples to examine their hearts when they pray and to repent of any unforgiveness they may be holding against someone else. "If, when you pray," He says, "and you have grudges or bitterness toward another, forgive him." Why?

So your heavenly Father *can* forgive you of any trespasses you have committed, your heart will be pure, and God can move on your behalf.

As believers, you should guard your heart diligently because from the heart flow the issues, or source, of life (Proverbs 4:23). The reference in this scripture is not only to the arteries which carry the blood to all parts of the body, but also to the evil and good deeds that come from the heart, or center, of man (see Mark 7:18-21). When you keep your heart from evil (unforgiveness), it is easy to obey God's commands and God promises to hear and answer your prayers:

> *If I regard iniquity in my heart, the Lord will not hear me: But verily God hath heard me; he hath attended to the voice of my prayer. Blessed be God, which hath not turned away my prayer, nor his mercy from me* (Psalms 66:18-20).

In Psalms 66 the psalmist knew his prayers *could not* be heard, much less answered, if sin was in his heart. He proclaimed that if "he" beheld sin in his own heart, God would turn away his prayer and it would bounce off heaven's walls. Judge yourself, therefore, before and during your prayer. Ask the Holy Spirit to reveal any areas of unforgiveness or unrepented sin. As He unfolds these areas to you, sincerely repent and then place your petitions before God.

Some of the quickest answers to prayer come when you ask God what you're doing wrong. God never told us to examine others; He said to examine our own hearts. Be sensitive to the Holy Spirit and, if He points to something specific, repent of it. As soon as you repent, He's forgiven you and wiped your slate clean—you can expect an answer to your prayer. The number-one thing, however, is to check to see if you have unforgiveness or some other iniquity in your heart.

A lack of dedication can also be a hindrance to answered prayer. Some people have an easier time praying than others because they have "given themselves" to prayer. They block out a certain time *each* day and don't allow anyone or anything to interfere with their fellowship with God. Others pray only occasionally or as the need arises. Practice makes perfect, so as you begin praying more consistently, you will develop an intimacy with the Father. Your communication to Him will begin to flow with ease and you will experience more—and faster—answers to your prayers.

Lack of faith, or doubt, is another heaven stopper. James 1:7,8 says a person who waivers in faith is unstable and will not receive an answer from God. When your faith is at a low ebb or you feel weary, find someone to stand with you as Aaron and Hur did with Moses (see Exodus 17:12). The scripture says one shall put a thousand to flight, and two shall put ten thousand; so as the two of you enter into a prayer of agreement, you will release a double portion of faith and the power of that faith guarantees God will answer.

Harmony is extremely important in the prayer of agreement, so you should be very selective when you choose someone to stand in faith with you. Not every Christian will understand where your level of faith is (or isn't) and may have a hard time standing with you. Ask the Holy Spirit for a prayer partner who will agree in prayer with you during your times of need.

A wrong or selfish motive can prevent an answer to prayer. James 4:2,3 says you can ask in prayer and not receive an answer because you are praying amiss. David fasted and prayed for the life of his son who was born out of his adulterous relationship with Bath-sheba. Although he repented of his sin, God could not honor David's prayer and the infant died (see II Samuel 12:15-18). Another example of wrong or selfish motives is praying that you'll win the lottery or for a person to die so you can marry his or her spouse.

When I was just starting out in ministry, someone gave me a flier advertising an international women's convention. I said, "God, let them invite me. It would be a real plum to get an invitation to that event."

I was not invited to speak at the convention that

year, but two years later I received an invitation. God had dealt with me in the interim about His call on my life. Although this was a big, international women's convention, God had told me when I first started traveling that He didn't want me to speak to women's groups.

"Why?" I had asked Him.

"Because I have called you to 'cover the earth with My Word.' If you go to women's groups, you'll be labeled as a woman's speaker, and that's not My call on your life."

Now I speak to women's groups, but Marilyn Hickey Ministries is long-term and well-established. At the beginning, God absolutely told me, "No." Yet I had prayed for the invitation to speak before I knew or understood His call for me.

When they called and extended the invitation for me to speak, my first reaction was, "Yes!" But I had a bad feeling when I hung up the phone. I asked God, "What's wrong with me? I don't have any joy about this."

"You will have an invitation from every women's group in the United States," God answered. "You'll have to write a thousand letters to say, 'No.' The reason you want that invitation is because of your ego."

I agreed with Him and gladly called them back and said, "You need a speaker who has the vision and call for your ministry. I love your ministry, but

I do not feel like God has given me that part of His great harvest to minister to." They were very sweet and released me and got a much better speaker than I would ever have been because God hadn't called me to minister to them.

Sometimes we pray for selfish reasons. Ask God if your motive is wrong. If He says, "Yes," repent and change the direction of your prayer. We have all prayed selfishly at one time or another.

A lack of compassion is another hindrance to prayer. Faith and God's love go hand-in-hand (see Galatians 5:6). When you walk in forgiveness and the love of God, His compassion will flow through you and your faith will be released to believe for the impossible. If you are a person who, by nature, does not "like people," make a decision to extend God's love and compassion to others. Only then can God pour His compassion out of you. Otherwise, your lack of compassion will be similar to a stopped-up sink—you'll have a backlog of unanswered prayers and God will be on the other end gurgling, but unable to answer you (see Proverbs 21:13).

Regardless of how great your need is, the prayers of a person who is without compassion for others, or constantly involved in strife and conflict will not be heard by God. A lack of domestic tranquility hinders the prayers of many married people. If you and your mate fight constantly or are always in strife with one another, it will affect your prayer life:

> *Likewise, ye husbands, dwell with them according to knowledge, giving honour unto the wife, as unto the weaker vessel, and as being heirs together of the grace of life; that your prayers be not hindered* (I Peter 3:7).

You may say, "I have an unsaved mate and it's hard to be in agreement." Although this may be true, you can dwell in peace with your spouse as much as possible. Strive for peace in your home and avoid strife as though it were a poisonous snake.

The Incubation Period

Let's go from hindrances to prayer to prevailing prayer—or what to do while you're waiting for an answer to come. Although some prayers are answered instantly, some go through an incubation period. The devil may torment you while you are standing in faith, waiting. If you're not careful, he will even try to steal your faith or try to convince you that God won't answer your prayers. Don't believe him!

James 5:17,18 says the prophet Elijah prayed earnestly and he was flesh and blood just as you are. Although Elijah had faults and weaknesses, his prayers caused the heavens not to rain. As you wait upon the Lord, stand on the Word of God, rehearse past victories God has given you, be

PATIENT, and cast not away your confidence in God's ability to move on your behalf (see Hebrews 10:35).

Chapter Nine
Early Morning Prayer

. . . those that seek me early shall find me (Proverbs 8:17).

In studying the scriptures on prayer, I discovered the Bible characters with the most tremendous prayer lives prayed early in the morning.

And they rose up in the morning early, and worshipped before the LORD, . . . (I Samuel 1:19).

Awake up, my glory; awake, psaltery and harp: I myself will awake early. I will praise thee, O Lord, among the people: I will sing unto thee among the nations (Psalms 57:8,9).

Job, who was considered to be an intercessor, prayed for his children early in the morning:

. . . Job sent and sanctified them, and rose up early in the morning, and offered burnt offerings according to the number of them all: . . . (Job 1:5).

Jesus prayed early in the morning, long before day break:

And in the morning, rising up a great while before day, he went out, and departed into

a solitary place, and there prayed
(Mark 1:35).

Early morning prayer is effective because it gives you a head start on your day and you are not yet contaminated with the things of the world. You are better prepared for what the day has in store after you've received your marching orders from Headquarters.

If you've noticed, dew settles on the grass early in the morning. When the sun comes up, the dew evaporates. I think the dew is often taught as a "type" of the presence of the Lord. In other words, there is a special presence of the Lord early in the morning. To get up early in the morning is to get the dew of His presence.

The Lord sent the Israelites manna early in the morning. If they waited until noon to gather it, they would be too late because the manna spoiled with the heat of the day.

I'm not saying you shouldn't pray in the middle of the day or late at night—in fact, I encourage you to pray as many times a day as possible. However, preventive prayer is always better than remedial prayer. You get a head start on the devil when you begin your day with prayer.

Begin each day with prayer and each week with prayer and fasting. Make a consecration now about how much you will pray and fast on a continual basis. Ask the Holy Spirit to show you how and what to pray for in every situation and be consistent! A consistent prayer life will keep you in a place of faith. And don't forget the twins— prayer and fasting! Keep them together and you will have one of the most effective and powerful prayer lives you've ever had. God will bless you as you discipline yourself to fast and seek him in supplications, prayers, intercessions, and giving of thanks on a consistent basis.

Daily Prayer Devotionals

The Call to Prayer

Seek ye the LORD while he may be found, call ye upon him while he is near (Isaiah 55:6).

Be careful for nothing; but in every thing by prayer and supplication with thanksgiving let your requests be made known unto God (Philippians 4:6).

God's Direction

Shew me thy ways, O LORD; teach me thy paths. Lead me in thy truth, and teach me: for thou art the God of my salvation; on thee do I wait all the day (Psalms 25:4,5).

But he that entereth in by the door is the shepherd of the sheep. To him the porter openeth; and the sheep hear his voice: and he calleth his own sheep by name, and leadeth them out. I am the good shepherd, and know my sheep, and am known of mine (John 10:2,3,14).

Salvation
For God so loved the world, that he gave his only begotten Son, that whosoever believeth in him should not perish, but have everlasting life. For God sent not his Son into the world to condemn the world; but that the world through him might be saved (John 3:16,17).

That if thou shalt confess with thy mouth the Lord Jesus, and shalt believe in thine heart that God hath raised him from the dead, thou shalt be saved. For with the heart man believeth unto righteousness; and with the mouth confession is made unto salvation. For the scripture saith, Whosoever believeth on him shall not be ashamed (Romans 10:9-11).

The Holy Spirit
And I will pray the Father, and he shall give you another Comforter, that he may abide with you for ever; Even the Spirit of truth; whom the world cannot receive, because it

seeth him not, neither knoweth him: but ye know him; for he dwelleth with you, and shall be in you (John 14:16,17).

But God hath revealed them unto us by his Spirit: for the Spirit searcheth all things, yea, the deep things of God (I Corinthians 2:10).

The Blood of Jesus
For the life of the flesh is in the blood: and I have given it to you upon the altar to make an atonement for your souls: for it is the blood that maketh an atonement for the soul (Leviticus 17:11).

And they overcame him by the blood of the Lamb, and by the word of their testimony; and they loved not their lives unto the death (Revelation 12:11).

Unsaved Loved Ones
Ask of me, and I shall give thee the heathen for thine inheritance, and the uttermost parts of the earth for thy possession (Psalms 2:8).

And they said, Believe on the Lord Jesus Christ, and thou shalt be saved, and thy house (Acts 16:31).

Christ Centered

My mouth shall speak the praise of the LORD; and let all flesh bless his holy name for ever and ever (Psalms 145:21).

Abide in me, and I in you. As the branch cannot bear fruit of itself, except it abide in the vine; no more can ye, except ye abide in me. I am the vine, ye are the branches: He that abideth in me, and I in him, the same bringeth forth much fruit: for without me ye can do nothing (John 15:4,5).

Finances

Bring ye all the tithes into the storehouse, that there may be meat in mine house, and prove me now herewith, saith the LORD of hosts, if I will not open you the windows of heaven, and pour you out a blessing, that there shall not be room enough to receive it. And I will rebuke the devourer for your sakes, and he shall not destroy the fruits of your ground; neither shall your vine cast her fruit before the time in the field, saith the LORD of hosts. And all nations shall call you blessed: for ye shall be a delightsome land, saith the LORD of hosts (Malachi 3:10-12).

Give, and it shall be given unto you; good measure, pressed down, and shaken together, and running over, shall men give into your bosom. For with the same measure that you mete withal it shall be measured to you again (Luke 6:38).

Witnessing
The fruit of the righteous is a tree of life; and he that winneth souls is wise (Proverbs 11:30).

Go ye therefore, and teach all nations, baptizing them in the name of the Father, and of the Son, and of the Holy Ghost: Teaching them to observe all things whatsoever I have commanded you: and, lo, I am with you alway, even unto the end of the world. Amen (Matthew 28:19,20).

Rejection
He healeth the broken in heart, and bindeth up their wounds (Psalms 147:3).

I will not leave you comfortless: I will come to you (John 14:18).

Loneliness
Blessed is the man that trusteth in the LORD,

and whose hope the LORD is. For he shall be as a tree planted by the waters, and that spreadeth out her roots by the river, and shall not see when heat cometh, but her leaf shall be green; and shall not be careful in the year of drought, neither shall cease from yielding fruit (Jeremiah 17:7,8).

And the peace of God, which passeth all understanding, shall keep your hearts and minds through Christ Jesus. Finally, brethren, whatsoever things are true, whatsoever things are honest, whatsoever things are just, whatsoever things are pure, whatsoever things are lovely, whatsoever things are of good report; if there be any virtue, and if there be any praise, think on these things (Philippians 4:7,8).

Sexual Purity
I beseech you therefore, brethren, by the mercies of God, that ye present your bodies a living sacrifice, holy, acceptable unto God, which is your reasonable service. And be not conformed to this world: but be ye transformed by the renewing of your mind, that ye may prove what is that good, and acceptable, and perfect, will of God (Romans 12:1,2).

If we confess our sins, he is faithful and just to forgive us our sins, and to cleanse us from all unrighteousness (I John 1:9).

Believing for a Mate
Wait on the LORD: be of good courage, and he shall strengthen thine heart: wait, I say, on the LORD (Psalms 27:14).

If ye abide in me, and my words abide in you, ye shall ask what ye will, and it shall be done unto you (John 15:7).

Preparing for Marriage
Therefore shall a man leave his father and his mother, and shall cleave unto his wife: and they shall be one flesh (Genesis 2:24).

But I would have you know, that the head of every man is Christ; and the head of the woman is the man; and the head of Christ is God (I Corinthians 11:3).

Parenting
And these words, which I command thee this day, shall be in thine heart: and thou shalt teach them diligently unto thy children, And shalt talk of them when thou sittest in thine house, and when thou walkest by the way,

and when thou liest down, and when thou risest up. And thou shalt bind them for a sign upon thine hand, and they shall be as frontlets between thine eyes. And thou shalt write them upon the posts of thy house, and on thy gates (Deuteronomy 6:6-9).

And, ye fathers, provoke not your children to wrath: but bring them up in the nurture and admonition of the Lord (Ephesians 6:4).

Unsaved Spouse
And they said, Believe on the Lord Jesus Christ, and thou shalt be saved, and thy house (Acts 16:31).

Likewise, ye wives, be in subjection to your own husbands; that, if any obey not the word, they also may without the word be won by the conversation of the wives; While they behold your chaste conversation coupled with fear (I Peter 3:1,2)

Desiring Children
He maketh the barren woman to keep house, and to be a joyful mother of children. Praise ye the LORD (Psalms 113:9).

Now faith is the substance of things hoped

for, the evidence of things not seen. But without faith it is impossible to please him: for he that cometh to God must believe that he is, and that he is a rewarder of them that diligently seek him. Through faith also Sara herself received strength to conceive seed, and was delivered of a child when she was past age, because she judged him faithful who had promised (Hebrews 11:1,6,11).

Unfaithful Husband

Deliver me out of the mire, and let me not sink: let me be delivered from them that hate me, and out of the deep waters. Let not the waterflood overflow me, neither let the deep swallow me up, and let not the pit shut her mouth upon me. Hear me, O LORD; for thy lovingkindness is good: turn unto me according to the multitude of thy tender mercies. And hide not thy face from thy servant; for I am in trouble: hear me speedily (Psalms 69:14-17).

Casting all your care upon him; for he careth for you. Be sober, be vigilant; because your adversary the devil, as a roaring lion, walketh about, seeking whom he may devour (I Peter 5:7,8).

Sexual Temptation

And he said, That which cometh out of the man, that defileth the man. For from within, out of the heart of men, proceed evil thoughts, adulteries, fornications, murders, Thefts, covetousness, wickedness, deceit, lasciviousness, an evil eye, blasphemy, pride, foolishness: All these evil things come from within, and defile the man (Mark 7:20-23).

Blessed is the man that endureth temptation: for when he is tried, he shall receive the crown of life, which the Lord hath promised to them that love him. Let no man say when he is tempted, I am tempted of God: for God cannot be tempted with evil, neither tempteth he any man: But every man is tempted, when he is drawn away of his own lust, and enticed. Then when lust hath conceived, it bringeth forth sin: and sin, when it is finished, bringeth forth death (James 1:12-15).

Overcoming Satan

Thou shalt not be afraid for the terror by night; nor for the arrow that flieth by day; Nor for the pestilence that walketh in darkness; nor for the destruction that wasteth at noonday. A thousand shall fall at thy side, and ten thousand at thy right hand; but it shall not come nigh thee (Psalms 91:5-7).

And he said unto them, I beheld Satan as lightning fall from heaven. Behold, I give unto you power to tread on serpents and scorpions, and over all the power of the enemy: and nothing shall by any means hurt you (Luke 10:18,19).

Jealousy
He that hath no rule over his own spirit is like a city that is broken down, and without walls (Proverbs 25:28).

Casting down imaginations, and every high thing that exalteth itself against the knowledge of God, and bringing into captivity every thought to the obedience of Christ (II Corinthians 10:5).

Fear
I sought the LORD, and he heard me, and delivered me from all my fears (Psalms 34:4).

For God hath not given us the spirit of fear; but of power, and of love, and of a sound mind (II Timothy 1:7).

Drudgery
The LORD bless thee, and keep thee: The LORD make his face shine upon thee, and be gracious unto thee: The LORD lift up his countenance upon thee, and give thee peace (Numbers 6:24-26).

That ye might walk worthy of the Lord unto all pleasing, being fruitful in every good work, and increasing in the knowledge of God (Colossians 1:10).

Job/Career
Be ye strong therefore, and let not your hands be weak: for you work shall be rewarded (II Chronicles 15:7).

Let all your things be done with charity (I Corinthians 16:14).

Healing for a Loved One
Fear thou not; for I am with thee: be not dismayed; for I am thy God: I will strengthen thee; yea, I will help thee; yea, I will uphold thee with the right hand of my righteousness (Isaiah 41:10).

Beloved, I wish above all things that thou mayest prosper and be in health, even as thy soul prospereth (III John 2).

Death of a Loved One
Thou wilt keep him in perfect peace, whose mind is stayed on thee: because he trusteth in thee (Isaiah 26:3).

I will not leave you comfortless: I will come to you. Peace I leave with you, my peace I give unto you: not as the world giveth, give I unto you. Let not your heart be troubled, neither let it be afraid (John 14:18,27).

Retirement
Enlarge the place of thy tent, and let them stretch forth the curtains of thine habitations: spare not, lengthen thy cords, and strengthen thy stakes (Isaiah 54:2).

Wherefore seeing we also are compassed about with so great a cloud of witnesses, let us lay aside every weight, and the sin which doth so easily beset us, and let us run with patience the race that is set before us (Hebrews 12:1).

Pregnancy
Lo, children are an heritage of the LORD: and the fruit of the womb is his reward (Psalms 127:3).

For thou hast possessed my reins: thou hast covered me in my mother's womb. I will praise thee; for I am fearfully and wonderfully made: marvellous are thy works; and that my soul knoweth right well. My substance was not hid from thee, when I was made in secret, and curiously wrought in the lowest parts of the earth. Thine eyes did see my substance, yet being unperfect; and in thy book all my members were written, which in continuance were fashioned, when as yet there was none of them (Psalms 139:13-16).

Childbirth
When thou passest through the waters, I will be with thee; and through the rivers, they shall not overflow thee: when thou walkest through the fire, thou shalt not be burned; neither shall the flame kindle upon thee (Isaiah 43:2).

I can do all things through Christ which strengtheneth me (Philippians 4:13).

Abortion
Thou shalt not kill (Exodus 20:13).

And they brought young children to him, that he should touch them: and his disciples rebuked those that brought them. But when Jesus saw it, he was much displeased, and said unto them, Suffer the little children to come unto me, and forbid them not: for of such is the kingdom of God. Verily I say unto you, Whosoever shall not receive the kingdom of God as a little child, he shall not enter therein. And he took them up in his arms, put his hands upon them, and blessed them (Mark 10:13-16).

A Sick Child
Who forgiveth all thine iniquities; who healeth all thy diseases (Psalms 103:3).

Who his own self bare our sins in his own body on the tree, that we, being dead to sins, should live unto righteousness: by whose stripes ye were healed (I Peter 2:24).

A Handicapped Child
I will seek that which was lost, and bring again that which was driven away, and will bind up that which was broken, and will strengthen that which was sick: . . . (Ezekiel 34:16).

Take heed that ye despise not one of these little ones; for I say unto you, That in heaven their angels do always behold the face of my Father which is in heaven (Matthew 18:10).

A Rebellious Child

Correct thy son, and he shall give thee rest; yea, he shall give delight unto thy soul (Proverbs 29:17).

Wherefore take unto you the whole armour of God, that ye may be able to withstand in the evil day, and having done all, to stand. Above all, taking the shield of faith, wherewith ye shall be able to quench all the fiery darts of the wicked (Ephesians 6:13,16).

Death of a Child

The LORD is good, a strong hold in the day of trouble; and he knoweth them that trust in him (Nahum 1:7).

Let not your heart be troubled: ye believe in God, believe also in me. In my Father's house are many mansions: if it were not so, I would have told you. I go to prepare a place for you. And if I go and prepare a place for you, I will come again, and receive you unto myself; that where I am, there ye may be also (John 14:1-3).

Godly Wisdom
When wisdom entereth into thine heart, and knowledge is pleasant unto thy soul; Discretion shall preserve thee, understanding shall keep thee (Proverbs 2:10,11).

If any of you lack wisdom, let him ask of God, that giveth to all men liberally, and upbraideth not; and it shall be given him (James 1:5).

Disciplining a Child
Chasten thy son while there is hope, and let not thy soul spare for his crying (Proverbs 19:18).

Now no chastening for the present seemeth to be joyous, but grievous: nevertheless afterward it yieldeth the peaceable fruit of righteousness unto them which are exercised thereby (Hebrews 12:11).

A Rejected Child
Hear my cry, O God; attend unto my prayer. From the end of the earth will I cry unto thee, when my heart is overwhelmed: lead me to

the rock that is higher than I. For thou hast been a shelter for me, and a strong tower from the enemy. I will abide in thy tabernacle for ever: I will trust in the covert of thy wings. Selah (Psalms 61:1-4)

And that we may be delivered from unreasonable and wicked men: for all men have not faith. But the Lord is faithful, who shall stablish you, and keep you from evil. And the Lord direct your hearts into the love of God, and into the patient waiting for Christ (II Thessalonians 3:2,3,5).

An Adult Child
To every thing there is a season, and a time to every purpose under the heaven: A time to weep, and a time to laugh; a time to mourn, and a time to dance; A time to cast away stones, and a time to gather stones together; a time to embrace, and a time to refrain from embracing; A time to get, and a time to lose; a time to keep, and a time to cast away (Ecclesiastes 3:1,4-6).

Not that I speak in respect of want: for I have learned, in whatsoever state I am, therewith to be content. I know both how to be abased, and I know how to abound: every where and

96

in all things I am instructed both to be full and to be hungry, both to abound and to suffer need (Philippians 4:11,12).

Teaching a Child About God

And they that be wise shall shine as the brightness of the firmament; and they that turn many to righteousness as the stars for ever and ever (Daniel 12:3).

And that from a child thou hast known the holy scriptures, which are able to make thee wise unto salvation through faith which is in Christ Jesus. All scripture is given by inspiration of God, and is profitable for doctrine, for reproof, for correction, for instruction in righteousness: That the man of God may be perfect, thoroughly furnished unto all good works (II Timothy 3:15-17).

Married Children

. . . a man of understanding holdeth his peace (Proverbs 11:12).

For this cause we also, since the day we heard it, do not cease to pray for you, and to desire that ye might be filled with the knowledge of his will in all wisdom and spiritual understanding; That ye might walk worthy of the Lord unto all pleasing, being fruitful in every good work, and increasing in the knowledge of God; Strengthened with all might, according to his glorious power, unto all patience and longsuffering with joyfulness (Colossians 1:9-11).

Grandchildren

Children's children are the crown of old men; and the glory of children are their fathers (Proverbs 17:6).

My little children, let us not love in word, neither in tongue; but in deed and in truth (I John 3:18).

Priorities

Blessed is the man that walketh not in the counsel of the ungodly, nor standeth in the way of sinners, nor sitteth in the seat of the scornful. But his delight is in the law of the LORD; and in his law doth he meditate day and night. And he shall be like a tree planted by the rivers of water, that bringeth forth his fruit in his season; his leaf also shall not wither; and whatsoever he doeth shall prosper (Psalms 1:1-3).

But seek ye first the kingdom of God, and

his righteousness; and all these things shall be added unto you (Matthew 6:33).

Separated From Loved Ones
For thou hast been a strength to the poor, a strength to the needy in his distress, a refuge from the storm, a shadow from the heat, when the blast of the terrible ones is as a storm against the wall (Isaiah 25:4).

And I will pray the Father, and he shall give you another Comforter, that he may abide with you for ever; Even the Spirit of truth; whom the world cannot receive, because it seeth him not, neither knoweth him: but ye know him; for he dwelleth with you, and shall be in you. I will not leave you comfortless: I will come to you (John 14:16-18).

To Renew Faith
He giveth power to the faint; and to them that have no might he increaseth strength. Even the youths shall faint and be weary, and the young men shall utterly fall: But they that wait upon the LORD shall renew their strength; they shall mount up with wings as eagles; they shall run, and not be weary; and they shall walk, and not faint (Isaiah 40:29-31).

Wherefore he saith, Awake thou that sleepest, and arise from the dead, and Christ shall give thee light (Ephesians 5:14).

Godly Example
Speak unto all the congregation of the children of Israel, and say unto them, Ye shall be holy: for I the LORD your God am holy (Leviticus 19:2).

Those things, which ye have both learned, and received, and heard, and seen in me, do: and the God of peace shall be with you (Philippians 4:9).

Diplomacy
A true witness delivereth souls: but a deceitful witness speaketh lies. He that is slow to wrath is of great understanding: but he that is hasty of spirit exalteth folly (Proverbs 14:25,29).

And the servant of the Lord must not strive; but be gentle unto all men, apt to teach, patient, In meekness instructing those that oppose themselves; if God peradventure will give them repentance to the acknowledging of the truth; And that they may recover themselves out of the snare of the devil, who are taken captive by him at his will (II Timothy 2:24-26).

Murmuring
Behold, all they that were incensed against thee shall be ashamed and confounded: they shall be as nothing; and they that strive with thee shall perish (Isaiah 41:11).

Dearly beloved, avenge not yourselves, but rather give place unto wrath: for it is written, Vengeance is mine; I will repay, saith the Lord (Romans 12:19).

Friendship
A man that hath friends must shew himself friendly: and there is a friend that sticketh closer than a brother (Proverbs 18:24).

Now I beseech you, brethren, by the name of our Lord Jesus Christ, that ye all speak the same thing, and that there be no divisions among you; but that ye be perfectly joined together in the same mind and in the same judgment (I Corinthians 1:10).

Quiet Time
And I said, Oh that I had wings like a dove! for then would I fly away, and be at rest.

I would hasten my escape from the windy storm and tempest (Psalms 55:6,8).

Come unto me, all ye that labour and are heavy laden, and I will give you rest. Take my yoke upon you, and learn of me; for I am meek and lowly in heart: and ye shall find rest unto your souls (Matthew 11:28,29).

Family Problems
Every wise woman buildeth her house: but the foolish plucketh it down with her hands (Proverbs 14:1).

But the wisdom that is from above is first pure, then peaceable, gentle, and easy to be intreated, full of mercy and good fruits, without partiality, and without hypocrisy (James 3:17).

Burnout
For I will pour water upon him that is thirsty, and floods upon the dry ground: I will pour my spirit upon thy seed, and my blessing upon thine offspring (Isaiah 44:3).

For which cause we faint not; but though our outward man perish, yet the inward man is renewed day by day (II Corinthians 4:16).

Overwhelming Responsibilities
And the LORD, he it is that doth go before thee; he will be with thee, he will not fail thee, neither forsake thee: fear not, neither be dismayed (Deuteronomy 31:8).

Be careful for nothing; but in every thing by prayer and supplication with thanksgiving let your requests be made known unto God. And the peace of God, which passeth all understanding, shall keep your hearts and minds through Christ Jesus (Philippians 4:6,7).

Exercise
By much slothfulness the building decayeth; and through idleness of the hands the house droppeth through (Ecclesiastes 10:18).

But I keep under my body, and bring it into subjection: lest that by any means, when I have preached to others, I myself should be a castaway (I Corinthians 9:27).

Diet
But Daniel purposed in his heart that he would not defile himself with the portion of the king's meat, nor with the wine which he drank: therefore he requested of the prince of the eunuchs that he might not defile

himself. Thus Melzar took away the portion of their meat, and the wine that they should drink; and gave them pulse. As for these four children, God gave them knowledge and skill in all learning and wisdom: and Daniel had understanding in all visions and dreams (Daniel 1:8,16,17).

And take heed to yourselves, lest at any time your hearts be overcharged with surfeiting, and drunkenness, and cares of this life, and so that day come upon you unawares (Luke 21:34).

Breaking Addictions

Then they cried unto the LORD in their trouble, and he delivered them out of their distresses. He sent his word, and healed them, and delivered them from their destructions (Psalms 107:6,20).

For the law of the Spirit of life in Christ Jesus hath made me free from the law of sin and death (Romans 8:2).

Divine Health

The LORD thy God in the midst of thee is mighty; he will save, he will rejoice over thee with joy; he will rest in his love, he will joy over thee with singing (Zephaniah 3:17).

But the Lord is faithful, who shall stablish you, and keep you from evil (II Thessalonians 3:3).

Healing
Ah Lord GOD! behold, thou hast made the heaven and the earth by thy great power and stretched out arm, and there is nothing too hard for thee (Jeremiah 32:17).

Is any sick among you? let him call for the elders of the church; and let them pray over him, anointing him with oil in the name of the Lord: And the prayer of faith shall save the sick, and the Lord shall raise him up; and if he have committed sins, they shall be forgiven him (James 5:14,15).

Aging
My flesh and my heart faileth: but God is the strength of my heart, and my portion for ever (Psalms 73:26).

And we know that all things work together for good to them that love God, to them who are the called according to his purpose (Romans 8:28).

Sleep

When thou liest down, thou shalt not be afraid: yea, thou shalt lie down, and thy sleep shall be sweet (Proverbs 3:24).

And the peace of God, which passeth all understanding, shall keep your hearts and minds through Christ Jesus. But my God shall supply all your need according to his riches in glory by Christ Jesus (Philippians 4:7,19).

Controlling Emotions

For wrath killeth the foolish man, and envy slayeth the silly one (Job 5:2).

If we live in the Spirit, let us also walk in the Spirit. Let us not be desirous of vain glory, provoking one another, envying one another (Galatians 5:25,26).

Depression

Remember ye not the former things, neither consider the things of old. I, even I, am he that blotteth out thy transgressions for mine own sake, and will not remember thy sins (Isaiah 43:18,25).

For as many as are led by the Spirit of God,

they are the sons of God. For ye have not received the spirit of bondage again to fear; but ye have received the Spirit of adoption, whereby we cry, Abba, Father. The Spirit itself beareth witness with our spirit, that we are the children of God (Romans 8:14-16).

Thought Life
For as he thinketh in his heart, so is he: . . . (Proverbs 23:7).

Rejoice in the Lord alway: and again I say, Rejoice. And the peace of God, which passeth all understanding, shall keep your hearts and minds through Christ Jesus (Philippians 4:4,7).

Deliverance From Evil Spirits
Is not this the fast that I have chosen? to loose the bands of wickedness, to undo the heavy burdens, and to let the oppressed go free, and that ye break every yoke? (Isaiah 58:6).

And I will give unto thee the keys of the kingdom of heaven: and whatsoever thou shalt bind on earth shall be bound in heaven: and whatsoever thou shalt loose on earth shall be loosed in heaven (Matthew 16:19).

Godly Self-Image

. . . Touch not mine anointed, and do my prophets no harm (Psalms 105:15).

There is therefore now no condemnation to them which are in Christ Jesus, who walk not after the flesh, but after the Spirit. The Spirit itself beareth witness with our spirit, that we are the children of God (Romans 8:1,16).

Overcoming Discouragement

Those that be planted in the house of the LORD shall flourish in the courts of our God (Psalms 92:13).

I am crucified with Christ: nevertheless I live; yet not I, but Christ liveth in me: and the life which I now life in the flesh I live by the faith of the Son of God, who loved me, and gave himself for me (Galatians 2:20).

Anger

Set a watch, O LORD, before my mouth; keep the door of my lips (Psalms 141:3).

For the wrath of man worketh not the righteousness of God (James 1:20).

Joy

But let all those that put their trust in thee rejoice: let them ever shout for joy, because thou defendest them: let them also that love thy name be joyful in thee (Psalms 5:11).

These things have I spoken unto you, that my joy might remain in you, and that your joy might be full (John 15:11).

Grief and Sorrow

He that goeth forth and weepeth, bearing precious seed, shall doubtless come again with rejoicing, bringing his sheaves with him (Psalms 126:6).

Let not your heart be troubled: ye believe in God, believe also in me. I will not leave you comfortless: I will come to you (John 14:1,18).

Guilt

And I will cleanse them from all their iniquity, whereby they have sinned against me; and I will pardon all their iniquities, whereby they have sinned, and whereby they have transgressed against me (Jeremiah 33:8).

There is therefore now no condemnation to

them which are in Christ Jesus, ... (Romans 8:1).

Thoughts of Suicide
Wait on the LORD: be of good courage, and he shall strengthen thine heart: wait, I say, on the LORD (Psalms 27:14).

For whosoever shall call upon the name of the Lord shall be saved (Romans 10:13).

Temptation
I call heaven and earth to record this day against you, that I have set before you life and death, blessing and cursing: therefore choose life, that both thou and thy seed may live (Deuteronomy 30:19).

Abstain from all appearance of evil (I Thessalonians 5:22).

Stress
He maketh the storm a calm, so that the waves thereof are still. Then are they glad because they be quiet; so he bringeth them unto their desired haven (Psalms 107:29,30).

There remaineth therefore a rest to the people of God. For he that is entered into his rest, he also hath ceased from his own works, as God did from his. Let us labour therefore to enter into that rest, lest any man fall after the same example of unbelief (Hebrews 4:9-11).

Friends
A friend loveth at all times, and a brother is born for adversity (Proverbs 17:17).

Owe no man any thing, but to love one another: for he that loveth another hath fulfilled the law (Romans 13:8).

Pride
Talk no more so exceeding proudly; let not arrogancy come out of your mouth: for the LORD is a God of knowledge, and by him actions are weighed (I Samuel 2:3).

But he that is greatest among you shall be your servant. And whosoever shall exalt himself shall be abased; and he that shall humble himself shall be exalted (Matthew 23:11,12).

Mental or Emotional Illness
Let this mind be in you, which was also in Christ Jesus (Philippians 2:5).

Receive Jesus Christ as Lord and Savior of Your Life.

The Bible says, *"That if thou shalt confess with thy mouth the Lord Jesus, and shalt believe in thine heart that God hath raised him from the dead, thou shalt be saved. For with the heart man believeth unto righteousness; and with the mouth confession is made unto salvation"* (Romans 10:9,10).

To receive Jesus Christ as Lord and Savior of your life, sincerely pray this prayer from your heart:

Dear Jesus,

I believe that You died for me and that You rose again on the third day. I confess to You that I am a sinner and that I need Your love and forgiveness. Come into my life, forgive my sins, and give me eternal life. I confess You now as my Lord. Thank You for my salvation!

Signed _____

Date _____

Write to us.
We will send you information to help you with your new life in Christ.

Marilyn Hickey Ministries • P.O. Box 17340
Denver, CO 80217 • (303) 770-0400

Prayer Requests

Let us join our faith with yours for your prayer needs. Fill out the coupon below and send to Marilyn Hickey Ministries, P.O. Box 17340, Denver, CO 80217.

Prayer Request _____

_____

_____

_____

_____

_____

Mr. & Mrs.   Please Print.
Mr.
Miss
Name Mrs. _____

Address _____

City _____

State _____Zip _____

Phone (H) (   ) _____

    (W) (   ) _____

If you want prayer immediately, call our Prayer Center at (303) 796-1333, Monday-Friday, 4 a.m. - 4:30 p.m. (MT).

BOOKS BY MARILYN HICKEY

A Cry for Miracles ($5.95)
Acts of the Holy Spirit ($9.95)
Angels All Around ($9.95)
Armageddon ($4.95)
Ask Marilyn ($9.95)
Be Healed ($9.95)
Bible Can Change You (The) ($12.95)
Book of Revelation Comic Book (The) ($3.00)
Break the Generation Curse ($9.95)
Daily Devotional ($7.95)
Dear Marilyn ($7.95)
Devils, Demons, and Deliverance ($9.95)
Divorce Is Not the Answer ($7.95)
Especially for Today's Woman ($14.95)
Freedom From Bondages ($7.95)
Gift Wrapped Fruit ($2.95)
God's Covenant for Your Family ($7.95)
God's Rx for a Hurting Heart ($4.95)

Hebrew Honey ($14.95)
How to Be a Mature Christian ($7.95)
Know Your Ministry ($4.95)
Maximize Your Day . . . God's Way ($7.95)
Names of God (The) ($7.95)
Nehemiah--Rebuilding the Broken Places in Your Life ($7.95)
Next Generation Blessings (The) ($9.95)
No. 1 Key to Success--Meditation (The) ($4.95)
Release the Power of the Blood Covenant ($4.95)
Satan-Proof Your Home ($9.95)
Save the Family Promise Book ($14.95)
Signs in the Heavens ($7.95)
What Every Person Wants to Know About Prayer ($4.95)
When Only a Miracle Will Do ($4.95)
Your Miracle Source ($4.95)
Your Total Health Handbook-- Body • Soul • Spirit ($9.95)

MINI-BOOKS: $1⁰⁰ each
by Marilyn Hickey

Beat Tension
Bold Men Win
Bulldog Faith
Change Your Life
Children Who Hit the Mark
Conquering Setbacks
Don't Park Here
Experience Long Life
Fasting and Prayer
God's Benefit: Healing
God's Seven Keys to Make You Rich
Hold On to Your Dream
How To Become More Than a Conqueror
How To Win Friends
I Can Be Born Again and Spirit Filled

I Can Dare To Be an Achiever
Keys to Healing Rejection
Power of Forgiveness (The)
Power of the Blood (The)
Receiving Resurrection Power
Renew Your Mind
Solving Life's Problems
Speak the Word
Standing in the Gap
Story of Esther (The)
Tithes • Offerings • Alms • God's Plan for Blessing You
Turning Point
Winning Over Weight
Women of the Word

WORD
to the
WORLD
COLLEGE

Explore your options and increase your knowledge of the Word at this unique college of higher learning for men and women of faith. Word to the World College offers **on-campus and correspondence courses** that give you the opportunity to learn from Marilyn Hickey and other great Bible scholars. WWC can help prepare you to be an effective minister of the gospel. Classes are open to both full- and part-time students.

For more information, complete the coupon below and send it to:

- - - - - - - - - - - - - - - -

Word to the World College
P.O. Box 17340
Denver, CO 80217
(303) 770-0400

Mr.
Mrs.
Please print.
Name Miss_____

Address _____

City _____ State _____ Zip _____

Phone (H) _____ (W) _____

For Your Information
Free Monthly Magazine

☐ Please send me your free monthly magazine, OUTPOURING (including daily devotionals, timely articles, and ministry updates)!

Tapes and Books

☐ Please send me Marilyn's latest product catalog.

Mr. & Mrs.
Mr.
Miss   Please print.
Name Mrs. _____

Address _____

City _____

State _____ Zip _____

Phone (H) ( ) _____

    (W) ( ) _____

Mail to:
Marilyn Hickey Ministries
P.O. Box 17340
Denver, CO 80217
(303) 770-0400

Covering the Earth with His Word!

Ministering to both physical as well as spiritual needs is at the heart of Marilyn Hickey Ministries and Marilyn's call to "cover the earth with the Word" in the uttermost parts of the world in places such as . . .

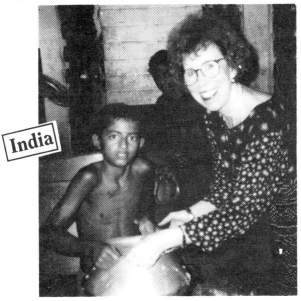

India